12 GREAT TIPS ON
WRITING TO INFORM

by Jeanne Marie Ford

12 STORY LIBRARY

12-Story Library is an imprint of Peterson Publishing Company and Press Room Editions.

Produced for 12-Story Library by Red Line Editorial

Photographs ©: Fuse/Thinkstock, cover, 1; Janice Richard/iStockphoto, 4; EVAfotografie/iStockphoto, 5; Diego Barbieri/Shutterstock Images, 6; Monkey Business Images/Shutterstock Images, 8; Steve Debenport/iStockphoto, 9, 16, 18; Silvia Jansen/iStockphoto, 10; Mark Bowden/iStock/Thinkstock, 11; Nicolas McComber/iStockphoto, 12; PeopleImages/iStockphoto, 13, 28; Alina Solovyova-Vincent/iStockphoto, 14; Georgios Kollidas/Shutterstock Images, 17; Yuri Kravchenko/Shutterstock Images, 19; harmpeti/iStockphoto, 20; g-stockstudio/Shutterstock Images, 21; Lucky Business/Shutterstock Images, 22; Tyler Olson/Shutterstock Images, 23; Digital Vision/Thinkstock, 24; Volt Collection/Shutterstock Images, 25; Christin Lola/Shutterstock Images, 26, 29; Vitchanan Photography/Shutterstock Images, 27

Library of Congress Cataloging-in-Publication Data
Names: Ford, Jeanne Marie, 1971- author.
Title: 12 great tips on writing to inform / by Jeanne Marie Ford.
Other titles: Twelve great tips on writing to inform
Description: Mankato, MN : 12-Story Library, 2017. | Series: Great tips on
    writing | Includes bibliographical references and index.
Identifiers: LCCN 2016002327 (print) | LCCN 2016004536 (ebook) | ISBN
    9781632352781 (library bound : alk. paper) | ISBN 9781632353283 (pbk. :
    alk. paper) | ISBN 9781621434467 (hosted ebook)
Subjects: LCSH: English language--Rhetoric--Juvenile literature. | Exposition
    (Rhetoric)--Juvenile literature.
Classification: LCC PE1429 .F68 2016 (print) | LCC PE1429 (ebook) | DDC
    808/.042--dc23
LC record available at http://lccn.loc.gov/2016002327

Printed in the United States of America
Mankato, MN
May, 2016

Access free, up-to-date content on this topic plus a full digital version of this book. Scan the QR code on page 31 or use your school's login at 12StoryLibrary.com.

Table of Contents

Determine Your Purpose

If you have ever written a report, a recipe, a holiday wish list, or even a "Keep Out" note to your sibling, you have written to inform. Most essays for school also involve informing in some way. Writing to inform helps readers learn more about a topic or process.

You might be writing for an assignment. If so, the first thing to do is to review the instructions

Writing thank-you cards is a simple way of writing to inform.

- Informational writing involves informing or explaining to the reader.
- If you are writing for an assignment, read the instructions carefully.
- Know your purpose. Keep it in mind as you write.

There are many different reasons for writing to inform. Your purpose is the force that will drive your writing. Every sentence you write will work toward your purpose.

Writing directions is also a way of informing.

carefully. Keep in mind what your teacher expects of the essay. How long should it be? What kind of research will you need to do? What questions should you ask before you begin?

Maybe you are not writing for an assignment. Think about what you want to accomplish. You might be writing a thank-you note for a gift you received. Your main purpose in this situation is to tell someone you are thankful. You might then explain how you plan to use the gift. Maybe you are writing directions to your house for your friends. You just want to get them from their homes to yours.

Connect with Your Topic

If you do not care about your subject, it is hard to make your readers care about it. Sometimes your teacher will give you a topic to write about. You might already know something about the subject. It might even be something you are interested in. But what if you are not?

No matter what your topic, it is good to find a personal connection to it. Maybe you have to write about the Winter Olympics, but you dislike sports and hate cold weather. Instead, you love ballet. Then you learn about the sport of ice dancing. You realize you have found something you are happy to write about.

On the other hand, your assignment may allow you to pick a topic. Sometimes, having a lot of freedom makes it difficult to decide where to start. Brainstorming is one way to come up with ideas you care about. Jot down a list of topics that come to mind. Once you have your list, look back at the assignment. Figure out which topic seems to work best for your purpose. What are you most interested in writing

If you are given an assignment, try to find a topic you are interested in, such as ice dancing.

Rules of Ice Dancing
- What types of dances are done?
- How are they scored?
- What moves are not allowed?

Creating a web is a good way to see how your thoughts fit together.

Ice Dancing

Ice Dancing vs. Pairs Skating
- What do ice dancers do?
- What do pairs skaters do?
- Similarities? Differences?

History of Ice Dancing
- How did the sport start?
- What kind of training is required?
- Where is it most popular?

about? Do you think you will be able to find enough information? If not, you may need to move on to another choice.

After you have settled on your general topic, you will need to narrow it down to something you can cover in one essay. Now it is time for more brainstorming. Ask questions to figure what information you want to

include. You might draw a web with your topic in the center. Doing this can help you organize your thoughts.

Quick Tips

- Choose a topic you care about.
- If you cannot choose your own topic, figure out why you care about the assigned topic.
- Ask questions to find out what you will cover.

Gather Reliable Information

Before you sit down to begin writing, you need information. Think about what you already know and what you still need to know about your topic. Then, decide where you can find facts to fit your purpose. Some topics will not require you to do any research at all. For example, perhaps you are asked to describe a process that you do every day. You are already an expert. You do not need to look for outside sources.

Other essays require research. The library is usually the best place to start. Library computers have access to large catalogs of information and books. Use keywords, or words associated with your topic, to begin your research. If you have trouble finding enough information, try different search terms. For example, if a search for "ice dancing" gives too few results, try "figure skating" or "Winter Olympics." Ask a librarian if you need help.

The Internet contains a huge amount of information. But you cannot believe everything you read online. Many websites contain information that is inaccurate or out of date. Make sure you are using reliable sources by asking yourself

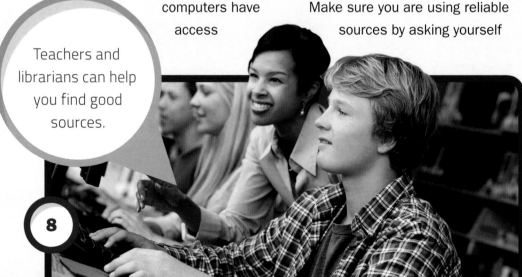

Teachers and librarians can help you find good sources.

TRY IT OUT

Take notes on this chapter. Write out the five most important points. Be sure to include both direct quotations and summaries.

Quick Tips

- Gather information before you begin to write.
- Make sure your sources are reliable.
- Take careful notes.

a series of questions. Is the author a professional writer or an expert in the field? Is the information current? Is the author's purpose to inform? Does the information you have found support your thesis? If you can answer "yes" to all of these questions, then you have found a good source.

Sometimes, you will be your own researcher. For example, you might be conducting an experiment. You may be the only primary source for the information. Primary sources are people who witness an event. They can also be documents from the period you are writing about. Secondary sources, such as most nonfiction books, get their information from primary sources. Sometimes, you will need to interview primary sources in order to write your essay. As you talk with a source, it is important to take careful notes or record the interview. Good note-taking will be a big help as you begin to write.

When writing a lab report, you may be the primary source.

4

Decide on Your Main Point

You have finally found enough information that you feel ready to begin writing. Later, if you find you need more, you can always go back to the library. Now it's time to figure out exactly what you want to say about your chosen topic. Your thesis statement is one sentence that tells the reader the essay's main point. As you write your rough draft, your thesis might change. But for now, this sentence will guide your writing plan.

As you develop your thesis, think again about your purpose. Think about the information you have gathered. A good thesis does not just introduce your topic. It also makes a claim. Instead of saying, "Ice dancing and pairs skating are both winter sports," you might try, "Ice dancing and pairs skating have many similarities and differences." Now be even more specific. How are they similar and different? What point do you want to make?

A thesis statement combines your research into one sentence.

A revised thesis might look like this: "While ice dancing might seem to require less athleticism, it is just as much of a sport as pairs skating." Remember, a thesis statement should always be a statement and not a question.

Make sure you will be able to support your claim with facts and evidence. For example, "Ice dancing is boring" is not a good thesis. It is an opinion that cannot be proven.

The thesis statement should appear toward the beginning of your essay, usually at the end of your introductory paragraph. Do not

> Writing a good thesis statement can take time.

announce what you plan to do in your essay: "In this essay I will write about ice dancing." Instead, simply state what your main point is.

A strong thesis will help you organize your essay effectively. Remember that every sentence should help support your thesis.

Quick Tips

- Develop a working thesis statement before you begin writing.
- Your thesis statement should make a claim and give the purpose of the essay.
- Place your thesis statement in the introduction of your essay.

5

Consider Your Audience

If you are writing an essay for an assignment, your teacher may be its only reader. Other times, you might have a bigger audience. You might be writing for the school newspaper. The entire student body may read your piece. Many decisions you make about your writing depend on the audience.

You will have to figure out what your audience knows about the topic. You do not want to spend the whole essay telling them what they already know. On the other hand, you do not want to confuse them by not giving enough information. For example, imagine you are writing an explanation of how you solved a math problem. You will not need to show that two plus two equals four. On the other hand, you cannot leave out the logic behind major steps of the problem.

Some essays will require a more formal style and tone than others. You might be writing about your

You may write differently for your teacher than for your friends.

Background information sets up readers to understand what you are saying.

own experiences. In this case, your writing will sound more conversational. It will sound more like you speak. You can include contractions, dialogue, and even humor. But if you are writing a research essay, you will probably want to use more formal language.

Formal essays also tend to avoid using the first person and the second person. First-person writing uses words such as *I*, *me*, and *my*. Second-person writing uses words such as *you* and *your*.

Quick Tips

- Figure out who your audience will be.
- Decide what information they need to know.
- Choose a tone that will work for your purpose and your readers.

TRY IT OUT

Write a letter to an elderly relative explaining how to use a certain type of technology. How would you text your friend the same information? How would you tell a young child? How are these three versions different?

6

Make a Plan

Now that you have decided on your main point, you might be tempted to dive right in and start writing. But it's a good idea to plan the structure of your essay first. An essay usually consists of an introductory paragraph, body paragraphs, and a conclusion. It will also need a title.

Your purpose will help you to figure out how many body paragraphs you need and how to organize them. You might have to tell about a process or describe an event or compare two things. Perhaps you will have to use a combination of these approaches.

Each body paragraph should begin with a topic sentence. The topic sentence states the main point of the paragraph. It is like the thesis statement of a paragraph. Every topic sentence should support the essay's

Imagining your audience can help you structure your essay.

Quick Tips

- Decide how you want to organize your essay.
- Use your thesis statement to develop topic sentences.
- Map out your essay's structure before you begin writing.

organizer, which is similar to an idea web. Or you might list your ideas and supporting details in an outline format. Each section of your outline will be about one main idea. These sections will become full paragraphs in your rough draft.

main point. But it should not repeat language from your thesis statement.

A chronological organization tells about an event from beginning to end. When writing about an experience or process, this is usually the best approach. You can also organize your essay using the spatial method. The spatial method groups information by location. This method is helpful when describing places. A third way to structure an essay is to arrange supporting details from least to most important.

If you are a visual thinker, you might want to try mapping your ideas on the page. Try using a graphic

OUTLINE

Working Thesis: Yorkshire terriers have many qualities that make them good pets.

Paragraph 1: Yorkies are small and easy to take care of. They do not
- need much food
- need much exercise
- need much space

Paragraph 2: Some people do not like Yorkies because they
- are aggressive
- are hard to housebreak
- need lots of grooming

Paragraph 3: But I love my Yorkie because it is
- smart
- loving
- adorable

Conclusion: A Yorkie is not the right pet for everyone, but mine is the perfect pet for me.

Catch the Reader's Attention

You are finally ready to begin writing your paper. Where do you start? The job of your first paragraph is to introduce your topic and hook your readers. This is also the place to give readers basic information about your topic before you get to your own point.

Let's say you are writing about President George Washington. You don't want to start with information that is too obvious or vague. For example: "George Washington is an important figure in United States history" is not telling the reader anything new.

Open your essay with something that will get your readers to want to learn more.

There are many interesting ways to grab a reader's attention. You might begin with a story: "On the day he became the first US president, George Washington had a terrible toothache." Or you could use a quotation: "'I cannot tell a lie,' George Washington famously said." Or you could share a surprising fact: "The story of George Washington chopping down his father's cherry tree was probably not true."

Your opening will lead into your thesis statement, which will introduce the rest of your essay. It may take time to think of an interesting opening. Skip the introduction if you are feeling stuck. Come back to it later. Start instead with your thesis statement and body paragraphs. The introduction often flows more easily after you have written the rest of your draft.

George Washington

TRY IT OUT

Suppose you are writing an essay about a family member. Craft a hook that will grab readers' attention.

Quick Tips

- Find a hook to interest your reader.
- Lead into your thesis statement.
- If you are stuck, come back to your introduction later.

Be Specific

As you write your body paragraphs, remember you should use several types of evidence. This includes facts, examples, definitions, and quotations. If you were writing about your favorite quarterback, you would want to give the player's statistics. You might mention he helped his team win a Super Bowl. But you need more vivid details to make the essay interesting. Try describing a memorable play he made. Quote a

Essays about athletes should include more than statistics.

Even if you are writing about your dog, make sure your facts are supported by research.

teammate who thinks highly of him. Don't tell your readers what a great player he is. Use the evidence to show them.

Every claim you make should be supported by research. For example, you might be writing about dogs. You might think it is safe to assume that all dogs bark. But after doing some research, you realize that the Basenji is a breed of dog that does not bark. Checking your facts helps you make sure you are not giving readers wrong information. It might also teach you something new.

Avoid clichés in your writing. These are expressions that have been used too often. They have lost their effect. If you are writing about a person you admire, don't say, "She would do anything for me," which is a cliché. Instead, describe a time when the person did something extraordinary.

Quick Tips

- Use many types of evidence in your writing.
- Use specific support for every claim you make.
- Avoid clichés.

TRY IT OUT

Write a description of the process of tying your shoes. Have a friend follow your instructions. Did it work?

Insert Information Smoothly

If you are writing a paper that involves research, you will use a combination of your own ideas and evidence from your sources. There are three ways to include research in your paper. The first is to quote your source. You should do this only when the quotation is important or cannot be said better in your own words. Quotations should be short. They should not be used to make your essay longer. Always copy the original text exactly. Use quotation marks around the quoted words.

The second way to bring research into your writing is to paraphrase.

Paraphrasing means putting the author's ideas into your own words. Make sure you paraphrase the writer's thoughts accurately. But your words need to be different from the original material. Simply moving or deleting a few words is not enough. Try to set the author's words aside as you paraphrase. Think about what is being said. Make the language your own.

Summarizing is the third way of adding research into your writing. A summary is a shorter form of a paraphrase. You might summarize a paragraph, a chapter, or even

Using a recording device during an interview can help ensure you use accurate quotes.

Quick Tips

- Decide when to quote, paraphrase, and summarize.
- Accurately present others' words and ideas.
- Introduce information from sources, and connect it to your thesis.

INSERTING QUOTATIONS

Introducing quotations helps readers know who said the words. It is good to respond to the quoted material in the next sentence:

> According to veterinarian Jane Smith, "One of my Yorkie patients, Sparky, lived to be 20." Of course, most Yorkies will not grow as old as Sparky. But many people prefer to own small dogs because they tend to live longer than larger ones.

a whole book in one or two sentences. Again, make sure you capture the true meaning of the source material in your summary.

Material taken from sources needs to transition naturally from your own writing. Introduce each quotation, paraphrase, or summary with a phrase that lets the reader know where the information came from. Then add your own thoughts to connect the source material to your thesis.

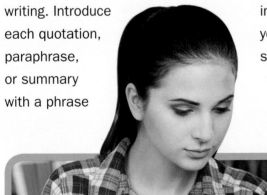

When paraphrasing, be sure to put things into your own words.

Give Your Sources Credit

Plagiarism is using someone else's words or ideas without giving them credit. It might be done on purpose or by accident. But it is always a serious issue. It could earn a failing grade on your essay. Of course, you cannot copy from a source and turn in the work as your own. You also cannot ask someone else to write your paper for you. But there are other forms of plagiarism that are not as obvious.

Quotation marks must be used to give credit to an author's words. If you do not use them where they are needed, you have plagiarized. A paraphrased passage that uses too much of the original source is also plagiarism.

If you use an author's ideas but not his or her exact words, you still need to show where you got the information. Citations give credit

Plagiarism is similar to cheating on a test.

SAMPLE BIBLIOGRAPHY

Citations include the author's name and title of the work. They are often placed in alphabetical order. Citations also include the work's publication information. This allows readers to find it easily. Here are two examples of citations:

Lunsford, Andrea A., and John J. Ruszkiewicz. *Everything's an Argument*. 6th ed. Boston: Bedford/St. Martin's, 2013. Print.

McWhorter, Kathleen T. *Successful College Writing: Skills, Strategies, Learning Styles*. 6th ed. Boston: Bedford/St. Martin's, 2015. Print.

for an author's ideas. There are many different ways to cite sources. You should follow your teacher's directions for creating a bibliography. This is a list at the end of your paper that shows all of the sources you used.

A bibliography gives credit to your sources.

Quick Tips

- Use quotation marks to give credit for an author's words.
- Use citations to give credit for an author's ideas.
- Provide a complete bibliography for any papers involving research.

Wrap It Up

Your conclusion is your last chance to drive home your point to your readers. You may have been taught that your conclusion should restate the main ideas in your essay. But this is not the case with more complex essays. This section needs to do more than repeat what you have just said. But it should not introduce any major new information.

It's important to take time to craft a good conclusion.

Quick Tips

- Make sure your essay has an interesting concluding paragraph.
- Do not introduce major information in your conclusion.
- Do not repeat what you have already said.

THINK ABOUT IT

Look at a piece you have written recently. What type of conclusion did you use? Do you like it? Try a different approach. Then try another. Which do you like best?

Balancing these two goals can be a challenge.

First, make sure you have a concluding paragraph. You do not want your paper to trail off without a good ending. If you restate your thesis in the conclusion, use different language. Try to avoid using unnecessary phrases like "in conclusion" or "lastly."

To wrap up on an interesting note, you might try using a fact, story, or quotation. You could also use your concluding paragraph to urge the reader to do something. Or you could show how your issue fits into the bigger picture. For example, if you

are writing a book report on a novel that is part of a series, you might indicate how this book leads into the next one.

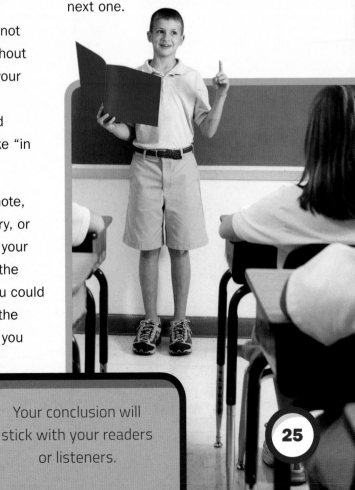

Your conclusion will stick with your readers or listeners.

12

Revise before You Edit and Proofread

Completing a rough draft feels great. But you are not finished yet. It's now time to go back and revise. Revision means looking at your piece with fresh eyes. Revising is not about editing sentences for spelling and grammar. It is about the ideas and structure of your whole essay. Now is the time to ask yourself some tough questions: Does every sentence in your paper support your thesis? Can you cut out any information? Have you used enough support for your main points? Have you given your sources credit? Do you use transitions to bring research into your paper smoothly? Are your introduction and conclusion interesting?

When you have finished your revision, you can turn to editing sentences. Now there is a new set of questions to ask: Does every sentence make sense? Can you cut out any words? Do you use the right words in the right places?

Revising sometimes means changing big parts of your essay.

TRY IT OUT

Write a paragraph about an important moment in your life. When you are finished, get a clean page and write about the same moment again. Try to re-see the whole story. Tell it in a completely different way. Which version do you like better?

Quick Tips

- Revise before you edit.
- Edit before you proofread.
- Be proud of your work!

to read your paper and give you suggestions.

You now have a final draft of your paper. You have worked hard. Take pride in what you have accomplished!

After editing, you should proofread for spelling, grammar, and punctuation. Use a spell-checker if you are writing on a computer. Try reading your essay out loud to make sure it flows well. If you can, get a friend

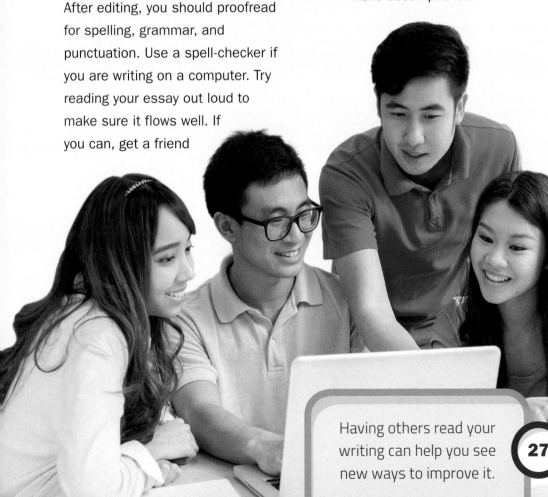

Having others read your writing can help you see new ways to improve it.

Writer's Checklist

✓ Connect with your topic.

✓ Write with your audience in mind.

✓ Figure out your main point before you begin writing.

✓ Plan the structure of your essay around your main point.

✓ Use reliable sources.

✓ Give your sources credit.

✓ Write an interesting introduction and conclusion.

✓ Mix research smoothly with your own ideas.

✓ Revise before you edit and proofread.

Glossary

audience
A person or group of people who read or listen.

bibliography
A list of sources you have used.

brainstorm
A method for thinking of ideas to write about.

chronological
Going from beginning to middle to end.

citation
Giving credit for someone else's ideas.

formal
Following an established form or set of rules.

interview
A meeting in which someone asks someone else questions.

nonfiction
Writing about real things, people, and events.

rough draft
An unfinished version of a piece of writing.

spell-checker
A computer program that finds and corrects writing errors.

statistic
A number that represents a piece of information.

tone
The feeling or attitude expressed by someone.

For More Information

Books

Bodden, Valerie. *Organized Essays*. Mankato, MN: Creative Education, 2011.

Bodden, Valerie. *Writing a Research Paper*. Mankato, MN: Creative Education, 2014.

Hubbard, Frances K., and Lauren Spencer. *Writing to Inform*. New York: Rosen, 2012.

Visit 12StoryLibrary.com

Scan the code or use your school's login at **12StoryLibrary.com** for recent updates about this topic and a full digital version of this book. Enjoy free access to:

- Digital ebook
- Breaking news updates
- Live content feeds
- Videos, interactive maps, and graphics
- Additional web resources

Note to educators: Visit 12StoryLibrary.com/register to sign up for free premium website access. Enjoy live content plus a full digital version of every 12-Story Library book you own for every student at your school.

Index

About the Author

Jeanne Marie Ford is an Emmy-winning TV scriptwriter and holds an MFA in Writing for Children from Vermont College. She has written numerous children's books and articles and also teaches college English. She lives in Maryland with her husband and two children.